When
Living
Hurts

A Publication
of the
YAD TIKVAH FOUNDATION

Sol Gordon, Ph.D.

WHEN LIVING HURTS

A lively *what to do book* for yourself or
someone you care about who feels
   discouraged ✦ *sad* ✦ *lonely* ✦ *hopeless* ✦
   angry or frustrated ✦ *unhappy or*
   bored ✦ *depressed* ✦ *suicidal*

FOR TEENAGERS
AND YOUNG ADULTS

Union of American Hebrew Congregations/New York

Library of Congress Cataloging-in-Publication Data

Gordon, Sol, 1923-
  When living hurts.

  Includes bibliographies.
  1. Youth—Suicidal behavior. 2. Suicide—
Prevention.   3. Adolescent psychology. I. Title.
HV6546.G67   1985   616.85'8445'05088055
85-20818
ISBN 0-8074-0310-5

Book design by Victoria Hartman

Acknowledgments

The following people have been helpful to me in developing this book: Rabbi Daniel B. Syme, Aron Hirt-Manheimer, Stuart L. Benick, Dr. Charles H. Haywood, Robert Young, Edward D. Miller, M.D., Julie Perlman, Lynn Leight, Craig Snyder, Gloria Blum, Judith and Josh Gordon, Jane Lanzen-dorf, Susan Gunther, Peter Watkinson, and Larry Bass, Ph.D.

I am also grateful to Rabbi Ramie Arian, James Hexter, Anita Saltz, Rabbi M. Robert Syme, Geraldine Voight, Mitchell Warren, Joy Weinberg, and Josette Knight.

This book was made possible in part by the members of the UAHC Northeast Lakes Council, through their generous gifts to the UAHC Fund for Reform Judaism.

I write for young people of all faiths, little faith, no faith, and for those still searching for a faith. I write to encourage you to stand for *something*; otherwise you may fall for anything.

"Believe that life is worth living and your belief
will help to create the fact."

—William James

"The secret of wisdom is kindness."

—Charles B. Haywood

ADVICE FROM A TEENAGER
WHO HAS ATTEMPTED SUICIDE
"No matter how bad things may seem,
they will get better. Just hold on."

"Nobody is weirder than anyone else—some people
just take longer to understand."

—Tom Robbins
Even Cowgirls Get the Blues

The great Jewish sage Hillel used to say
      "If I am not for myself, who will be for me?
      And if I am only for myself, what am I?
      And if not now, when?"
What do I think Hillel says to us now?
   There is an ever-present need to enhance ourselves and our spiritual aspirations but we must never forget our obligations to society lest we discover one day that it is too late.

   What does Hillel say to you?

A table of wisdom, worry, and what to do

xiii

When
Living
Hurts

Introduction

This is a book for teenagers and young adults who want to help people who are in trouble.

It is also for those who are themselves lonely, depressed, or suicidal.

Our basic message is that we are all our brothers' and sisters' keepers and that "living well" is the best antidote ("revenge") for feelings of hopelessness, helplessness, being unloved, unfairness, and tragedy. It focuses on how to cope appropriately with disappointments and imperfections (in an imperfect world).

Most other "how-to" books tell you

Not to worry. (When's the last time someone told you not to worry and you stopped?)

Not to feel guilty. (If you've done something wrong, why shouldn't you feel guilty?)

That you can be anything you want to be. (You should live so long.)

To get rid of unrealistic expectations. (How does one know in advance that one's expectations are unrealistic?)

That if you eliminate shoulds, musts, perfectionistic tendencies, worries, and other imperfections you'll be happy. (So, what else is new?)

The plain fact is that
   Life, in large part, is made up of things to worry about,
     not only personal things,
      but the state of the world,
         hunger, over-population, torture, crime-infested
         cities, disasters, personal tragedies, despair.

Life can be unfair, unlucky, uninteresting, unnerving
for large parts of the day
or for years.

Real people have bad moods,
periods of depression,
fall in love with someone who doesn't love them.

Life can also be full of joys, pleasures, and excitements. They
may not last long, but nevertheless they are real.

Most other self-help books want you to pretend that you are
the only reality. This book does not pretend. It acknowledges
the pain of the real world, but it also says that
   Optimism is easier than pessimism.
   Wisdom, daydreaming, and risk-taking introduce you to
     options that you never felt possible.

We don't have all the answers,
but we try to attend to many of your questions.
We expect you to make up your own mind,
especially about controversial issues
and in ways that enhance your own well-being.

If you or someone you know is suicidal

Fragments of an autobiography

Sometimes a present situation is grim. There is nothing one can do except allow (gracefully) the passage of time. My own childhood was filled with years of a schooling I hated, a loneliness I didn't understand, and parents I didn't appreciate. There were times when I lived with it, with some crying and trusting that some day.... I contemplated suicide and imagined how everybody would be sorry. It was hard not thinking about irrational ways out.

I began to feel better late in my teen years when I realized there is nothing wrong with being unhappy every once in a while. Lord knows there are lots of times and situations when unhappiness is the most appropriate response.

I figured out that it was not hard to tell when unhappiness has an important component of irrationality. That unhappiness comes equipped with symptoms like

     fear of high or closed places

     pains without disease—malfunctions or lesions

     chronic constipation

     gross loss of appetite

     sexual compulsions

that don't get you any place.

Rational unhappiness is mostly grand, dignified, private, a bit heroic, unselfish, free of irrational guilt or pride, and ends up being a learning experience.

How to get help urgently

If you're feeling really bad or thinking about suicide, you may not be in the mood to read a whole book. Read this part and after that turn immediately to the table of contents and read the brief sections that refer to you. Then confide in someone. Talk about what's troubling you. It is important, even if you have to reach out to several people before you get the response that gets you on track to feeling better. Try a friend—or a parent—first, even if you are sure they won't understand. Then get to an adult you can trust—a doctor, counselor, teacher, minister, rabbi—or call a crisis intervention center anytime, day or night. They will help you. (See list in Appendix.)

It's all right if you feel hopeless—just start out by saying, "Help me, I'm feeling really bad." This is the first step in getting better—finding someone who will know how to respond in the unique way that will reach you. By the way, it doesn't matter if you've tried this kind of advice before and it didn't help. This time it could. And, besides, time is on your side. In time you could change your mind about a lot of things.

Now, if it's someone you know who is in trouble—perhaps someone you care about has confided in you—turn immediately to the section, "What to do if someone you care about is suicidal" (page 13). Follow that with "Dying to live the good life?" (page 10).

If you feel the danger of suicide is imminent, don't leave the person alone. If possible, you or another person can call the police and report there is a suicide attempt in progress. Make sure you give the address and telephone number. Get as close to the person as he or she will allow and talk. "Let's talk. For my sake. It's important for me. If I can't persuade you not to kill yourself, you can go ahead with it later. Please, let's talk. It's possible that I don't understand how you feel. Explain it to me."

How to help someone who is in a panic or having what's sometimes called an anxiety attack

Anxiety is experienced as an overwhelming state of tension or fear (often in anticipation of some unknown danger, or in anticipation of not being able to handle a scheduled task or performance, which should not be confused with normal stress or tension before an event). Attacks may be accompanied by physical signs such as rapid heartbeat, sweating, trembling, nausea, difficulty catching your breath,* in addition to intense fears of losing control, going crazy, and even dying.

Here's what to do:

Say something like this—

"Listen, you are having an anxiety attack. If you've had one before, you know you'll get over it. If it's the first time, it's real scary. But it is not dangerous and it will pass. (How do you know? the person asks) I read about it in a book. (What causes it?) It's not important to figure it out now."

"Here's what you are supposed to do. Just sit down, close your eyes and tense up, then relax every part of your body. Start with your toes, feet, legs (then progressively move up and name the other body parts—suggesting that the person visualize the body parts in his or her mind)."

"I'll stay with you. Now listen—I know that all sorts of ideas will come into your mind. This is common. It happens to a lot of people. (How do you know?) It was clearly stated in this psychology book that I read. What you are going through is not comfortable (may even be terrifying) but it is not (I repeat, not) dangerous."

---

*If the person is panting and out of breath, one way to help him or her stop is: Have the person place a small paper bag around the nose and mouth and breathe into the bag until the panting stops. Breathing the same air over and over for three or four minutes helps the person control the panting by increasing the carbon dioxide in their blood back to normal levels, calming them down.

Please note: This is a first-aid procedure. Don't try to talk them out of it by suggesting it's nothing to worry about. Nor will this relaxation approach solve the basic problem. If intense physical pain is present, emergency medical help may be indicated. If it does turn out to be, as you suspected, an anxiety attack, talking with a counselor or psychiatrist could be suggested at a later time.

When the acute phase is over, the two of you could decide together what's feasible for now or what to postpone for another time.

IT'S A GOOD FEELING
WHEN YOU KNOW
WHAT TO DO
TO HELP SOMEONE IN TROUBLE

Dying to live the good life?

Depressed sometimes? *Everybody*—but everybody—gets depressed every once in a while. Almost all occasional depressions are normal. Have you ever thought about suicide? Did you know that almost everyone has?

About six thousand young people kill themselves every year. As a statistic by itself it makes no real impression. (How about if I told you that several hundred thousand teenagers make serious suicide attempts every year?)

Do you know someone who has killed himself (herself)? Probably yes. Isn't it painful to recall—to visualize—that person? Wouldn't you like to be in a position to help someone (or even yourself) who is seriously considering suicide?

First about depression: We live in a world that expects us to be happy (virtually all the time). Many parents say, "I don't care what you do with your life, as long as you are happy." (Of course, we are not always sure that they really mean it.) Ads in the media try to convince us that their products will make us happy. The truth of the matter is that life is not that way at all.

Life has many disappointments: deaths of people you love, tragic illnesses, prolonged periods of bad weather, betrayals, feelings of worthlessness and despair, times dominated by cries of "why me?" and wallowing in pools of self-pity. Most people discover ways of dealing with depression and become convinced that times will be better, even if at the moment of crisis it does not seem that way.

Normal depressions follow a bad event. Sometimes it may turn out that what was wrong was your perception—your way of looking at it. For example, your friend gave you the impression that he had deceived or compromised you—but then you discover it was not true.

Normal depressions don't last a "long" time. Normal

mourning can seem like an eternity, but during this time you allow your friends or parents to comfort you.

A more serious and what is commonly called a neurotic depression is usually related to accepting blame for something you didn't do, or feeling guilty for irrational reasons.

Sometimes, in response, people eat too much, use drugs or alcohol excessively—but it doesn't help. It only makes the depression last longer and get worse.

The most severe forms of depressions occur whether good or bad things happen. They can lead the body to function improperly. Significant changes in appetite and sleep are most common. This type of depression seems to have an organic base and can often be relieved with appropriate medication.

People who seriously consider, or do, commit suicide as a result of any of these depressed states haven't learned appropriate ways of dealing with disappointment. They feel there is no way out or that their agony will last forever. They feel there is no one who really believes in or understands them. For them, life is no longer meaningful. Many haven't understood that life without frustrations, depressions, and profound periods of mourning simply doesn't exist for anybody. But mostly it's inconceivable for them to imagine that

1. things always change
2. time heals
3. *YOU CAN FALL IN LOVE AT LEAST 18 TIMES!*

A lot of experts pretend they can describe a suicidal person, but they can't. Every person is unique and so are the reasons for wanting to end it all. Suicidal intent however is always a cry for help.

Anyone who is suicidal requires professional help and, sometimes, antidepressant medication. But psychiatrists, psychologists, and social workers can't "cure" a depressed person without the help of friends and family.

Let me convey a bit of personal philosophy that can be helpful. Don't go around looking for THE meaning of life.

**LIFE IS NOT A MEANING;
IT'S AN OPPORTUNITY
FOR MEANINGFUL EXPERIENCES.**

Disappointments are part of everybody's life.

Expect miracles in your life, otherwise you won't notice them when they happen.

The first miracle surfaces when you don't have to compare yourself to anybody else.

What to do if someone you care about is suicidal

Listen. Don't argue or attempt to prove that what he or she is doing doesn't make sense. Respond by saying things like—
  • I understand how you feel
  • As long as you are alive, things can change
  • I'll help and always stick with you
  • I care about you
Don't say:
  • You're being silly (or stupid)
  • Let's forget about it
  • Let's have some fun
  • Let's go to a movie, a dance.
Don't suggest drinking or drugs. By lowering inhibitions and muddying thinking, they make a person reckless or even could lead to suicide.

Don't be afraid to talk with your friend or brother or sister about what they are thinking about or planning to do. You could ask, "Have you ever felt like life's not worth living?" It's not that you are putting ideas into their heads—if they are considering suicide, it's good for them to talk about it. DIRECT QUESTIONS ABOUT SUICIDAL INTENT DO NOT PROVOKE SUICIDAL BEHAVIOR. First, ask them, "Have you ever wished you were dead?" "Are you thinking of suicide?" "Are there some things you've thought about or done that you've never told anyone?" Then find out how urgent the crisis is: "How do you plan to kill yourself?" "Have you bought . . . (the pills, knife, gun, etc.)?" "Have you been thinking about dying for a while now?" "When do you think you'll kill yourself?"

If the crisis is urgent (they know how they plan to die, have the means, and are ready to act) DO NOT LEAVE THEM. Go with them to a parent, a counselor, a minister, a rabbi, a suicide prevention clinic, whatever support system is best at the time. If the person refuses to meet with anyone, call someone secretly for help. YOU CANNOT BEAR THE BURDEN OF THAT RESPONSIBILITY ALONE.

If the suicidal thoughts are serious (remember: they should always be taken seriously) but not urgent, work with that person. Find out what's troubling them.

Usually, something has ignited a serious crisis: a rejection by a lover, the death of a friend, parents deciding to divorce, not being accepted by a college, poor grades, an unreasonable punishment from a parent or at school.

It doesn't matter if *you* think what they are upset about is trivial or not much in comparison to the troubles you have. It's how *they* feel that counts.

Accept the feelings. Don't tell them not to worry. Don't trivialize the event by saying things like "You'll get over it," "It's nothing," "You think you have troubles. . . ." Don't try to amuse them out of the hurt.

—Be a friend
    just
    sympathize
—Be sad with . . .
—Be with
—Go for walks
   (Don't sit around)
—Jog together
—Exercise with

—Don't take them to parties,
   or to be with people who are having fun.
Most really sad people become even more depressed when they are around people who are having a good time.

—Don't try to give easy answers or solve the problems all
   at once.
—Ask your friend:
   "Is this the worst thing that's ever happened?"

"What are some ways of dealing with it?"

Help the person list alternatives. Consider the following responses:

"I know you feel that there's no point in living without her (him), but it's well known that people can fall in love many times. It's not true that you can really fall in love only once. It's not fair to force another person to love you. What if someone you didn't love anymore tried to force *you* to love her (him)? Don't misunderstand me, I know it's hard, and it's o.k. to feel bad and be disappointed."

You might also say "It would be good if you would allow yourself to cry," or "I know your folks don't understand you. They care, but in their own way. When you have a family of your own, you'll do it differently."

Don't lay on a heavy guilt or religious trip.

Earl A. Grollman, in his excellent book *Suicide*, cautions that the

> potential suicide is already suffering from a heavy burden of punishing guilt feelings. One who speaks about suicide as an immoral act will not only block the possibility of further communication, but may actually contribute and advance the individual's present sense of discouragement and depression. For the suicidal person, self-destruction is not a theological issue, it is the result of unbearable emotional stress.

On the other hand, you might suggest "By killing yourself all you'll do is put a big guilt trip on everybody, your family, me." The main thing is for you to encourage your friend to talk, to reveal and confide.

Any suicidal intent or inference should be taken seriously. These inferences might include comments like:

- I won't be around much longer
- Soon nobody will have to worry about me
- I have nothing to live for
- Nothing works for me

Don't say things like:
  • You have everything going for you
Do respond with caring messages:
  • I appreciate how you feel
  • If you think I don't know how you feel, tell me more
about it, so I can understand you better
  • I know it sounds hopeless, but things can change—even
things that last a long time can change in minutes
Don't tell lies like:
  • She (he) really does love you
  • Everybody is your friend
Be a friend. Stay with the person as long as possible. Make a
definite appointment for the next visit. Say—

"Call me any time—even in the middle of the night." Go
out for a meal together, or an ice cream. The act of sharing a
meal can lift depression, if only for a while. Make a pact with
your friend: what she will do, what you will do, when you
will meet and compare notes. Let him know you will see him
through this.

And don't let your friend glorify death without respond-
ing: "Listen, pal, if you kill yourself, it's over. Only the
survivors suffer, and for the rest of their lives."

And besides, unconsciously, everyone who thinks about
suicide (listen, it's not unusual to think about it, even seriously) feels that they will be rescued at the last minute. Often
it doesn't happen and they die, or they botch up the attempt
and remain crippled for the rest of their lives.

With some depressions doctors can help. In some crisis
situations, it's surprising how a change in a parent's usual
response can bring immediate relief. What doesn't work is
blame, resentment, or hostility.

Convey that you care. Everybody needs someone who
believes in them. Respond to cries for "revenge" with:

  "Listen, my friend,
    there is only one revenge,
    and that is living well."

Nobody ever fully recovers from the guilt of a child or a close friend or sibling who commits suicide. There is always a dreadful feeling of "What did I do wrong?"

So many people who commit suicide, or think they want to, or try to, do so because of a sense of hopelessness, and sometimes because they feel life is without purpose or meaning. They may feel that threatening to kill oneself is heroic.

It is not heroic—it's a failure to connect meaningfully with people who could or would like to love and believe in them. Sure, your friend may need professional help as well. Be sure to tell your friend—not all therapists are good for every person. If you don't like or trust that professional the very first session, find someone else. There is nothing wrong with you if you don't like the first therapist who is available, no matter how important or famous that person is.

WHAT DO YOU DO IF YOU ARE TOLD IN CONFIDENCE THAT SOMEONE YOU CARE ABOUT IS THINKING ABOUT SUICIDE? DO YOU TELL ANYONE? YES! Find a way of telling his or her parents or a teacher or guidance counselor or minister or rabbi that you are worried. The more you are worried, the more explicit you should become.

You can't keep a suicidal intent confidential. Tell!

You can't always trust your own judgment about whether it's serious or not. You could easily be thinking:

- He is not the type
- Her carrying on is just an attention-getting device
- I can't believe she is serious
- He seems much better now

MANY SUICIDES ARE COMMITTED AFTER THE DEPRESSION HAS LIFTED AND THE PERSON HAS REGAINED THE ENERGY TO GO THROUGH WITH THE SUICIDE. She may have already decided to kill herself and therefore comes across as having nothing more to worry about. THIS CALM PERIOD MUST BE TREATED WITH URGENCY.

If your friend refuses to secure help, a starting point for you is calling a crisis center. Give him this book to read. Encourage her to tell a parent. He might start by showing parents the section of the book designed for them. You may have to tell a school counselor or, in a confidential way, one or both of your friend's parents.

Please realize that we're not expecting you to be the therapist and resolve the problem. At the same time, you may be the only person your friend confides in, and the only person who can help. By determining the seriousness of the crisis, motivating that person to seek help, and by showing your support, you can make a real difference.

If they say to you, "Leave me alone," you can be sure that they very seldom mean it.

THE CRUCIAL PART TO UNDERSTAND
IS THAT SUICIDAL INTENT IS ALWAYS TEMPORARY.
IT CAN BE REVERSED.

**Can you tell the difference between a cry for help,
a wish for attention, and depression?**

You can't always but here are some points to consider.

Francine Klagsbrun, in her excellent book for parents and counselors entitled *Too Young to Die—Youth and Suicide*, writes:

> Friends, relatives, teachers, co-workers . . . make up the front line of defense against suicide. . . . And, they must help, even if they believe the suicidal person is manipulating them or using threats of suicide to gain attention. A person who must resort to suicide to get attention has lost the ability to communicate in normal ways. *The person needs attention.* [Emphasis added.] Without it the next cry for help will be shriller, more desperate, more dangerous.

In any case, it's better to err on the side of concern than to be sorry later.

When you get right down to it, there are two main categories of suicides. The impulsive kind with no chance of return and the slow, not entirely intentional kind, often with equally grim results. The second kind may include:

Driving while intoxicated
Drug addiction
Heavy into alcohol
Dieting (to an extreme—sometimes called anorexia)
Smoking
Eating too much (when accompanied by self-induced regurgitation, it is called bulimia)
Suicide attempts
Sexual promiscuity
Violence and crime
Retreat into despair

Suicide warning signs

They could also be signs of depression, physical illness, a temporary, and even an appropriate, response to loss. They include:

Expressing feelings of hopelessness

Becoming uncommunicative

Having explosive outbursts

Loss of appetite or excessive eating

Losing interest in activities once considered enjoyable

Exhibiting loss of energy or extreme fatigue

Pacing relentlessly

Sleeplessness

A preoccupation with the notion that "nobody under-stands"

Talking about death

Running away from home

Moodiness and sudden bursts of crying

Increasing isolation from friends and family

A tendency to become more active and aggressive than usual (unlike suicidal adults who tend to become apathetic when severely depressed)

A serious drop in grades

Giving away a valued possession

Increased interest in getting his or her "life in order"

Talking about suicide

A sudden and intense interest in religious beliefs and the afterlife

A profound depression in response to recent loss, such as a divorce or death in the family, or a close friend moving away

A previous suicide attempt

Even though the vast majority of young people exhibiting one or more of the above signs will not attempt or commit suicide, or end up mentally ill, they do represent, for the most part, *changes* in behavior that warrant serious concern. Why take chances?

Here is something to think about:

> In some cases you may find yourself in the position of having to get direct help for someone who is suicidal and refuses to go for counseling. If so, do it. Don't be afraid of appearing disloyal. Many people who are suicidal have given up hope. They no longer believe they can be helped. They feel it is useless. The truth is, they *can* be helped. With time, most suicidal people can be restored to full and happy living. But when they are feeling hopeless, their judgment is impaired. They can't see a reason to go on living. In that case, it is up to you to use *your* judgment to see that they get the help they need. What at the time may appear to be an act of disloyalty or the breaking of a confidence could turn out to be the favor of a lifetime. Your courage and willingness to act could save a life.
>
> (Excerpted from *Suicide in Youth and What You Can Do about It.** Prepared by the Suicide Prevention and Crisis Center of San Mateo County, California in cooperation with the American Association of Suicidology and Merck Sharp & Dohme.)

"Whoever preserves one life, it is as if he preserved an entire world."
—*Scriptures*

---

*For free copies of this and other related publications, write to: Merck Sharp & Dohme, Health Information Services, West Point, Pennsylvania 19486.

Why are so many young people
killing themselves these days?

We don't really know. We do know that the suicide rate among young people aged 15 to 24 has tripled in the last 30 years resulting in between 5,000 and 6,000 deaths a year. In addition, several hundred thousand young people make serious suicide attempts every year. We do know that many of the suicides come from homes where there has been divorce or separation. But 13 million children under 18 have divorced parents. We would have to make the same comparisons for all the other reasons experts give:

Not getting along with parents

Drug and alcohol abuse

Overwhelmed by loss of parent or close friend

Feeling useless

Feeling unloved and unlovable

Rejection by a girlfriend or boyfriend

One expert, Charles H. Haywood,* challenges those who put most of the blame on parents:

> Suicide is an act of violence preceded in many disturbed individuals by feelings of hopelessness, helplessness and alienation, preoccupation with trivia, cynicism, inability to control moods, irregular and destructive health behavior patterns, absence of creative dreaming, unbearable loss or threat, and the availability of the means to kill oneself.

Dr. Haywood also believes uncontrollable rage, organic problems, hormonal imbalance may be factors in suicide. (A

---

*Charles H. Haywood is executive director of Crisis Intervention Institute in Buffalo, New York. Quoted from *The New York Times*, November 28, 1984.

complete medical evaluation is always indicated for people who are suicidal.)

The five characteristics most experts agree upon are the following:

1. Depression or a feeling of hopelessness are the most important factors in suicide.

2. Almost all are preventable.

3. Many teenagers who took their own lives declared in some way their intention of doing so. Suicide attempts of any kind should always be considered a "cry for help."

4. Almost all suicidal people have mixed feelings about it—they want to and they don't. Suicide is sometimes impulsive but it may also be an act of desperation or a wish for revenge.

5. Young people who kill themselves often feel that their families don't understand them. It usually comes at the end of a long period of multiple difficulties.

However much a young person feels intolerable emotion or unendurable pain, it will pass, it will change. It's temporary. When you get right down to it, each suicidal person is unique and each one is too young to die. As long as the person is alive, there is time for everything, including figuring out why he or she wanted out.

> *WHY DO SO MANY YOUNG PEOPLE*
> *WANT TO END IT ALL?*
> *WHAT'S THE RUSH?*
> *THEY'VE GOT A WHOLE LIFETIME*
> *AHEAD OF THEM.*

You really want to know in a few words? They haven't learned to cope with *disappointment*. We are a society that's into instant gratification. If they feel bad, they take a pill, a drink, they try to escape. If they can't get relief right away, their bad situation turns easily into despair.

Everybody has to learn to cope with disappointments and even tragic happenings. It's part of living.

If someone we love doesn't understand this, it's up to us to convince them. There is no greater *mitzvah** than to save a life.

"Although the world is full of suffering,
it is also full of the overcoming of it."
—Helen Keller

---

*Mitzvah is a Hebrew word which means a commandment but is usually translated as "good deed."

Are you dying to be the center of attention?

What's the point of being the center of attention if you are dead? You'll never know about it.

You think the only way to get your parents to listen to you is to make a suicide attempt. (You might actually die or botch up the job so you'll be crippled all your life.)

It's just not a good way of getting attention. Suicide is romantic only in novels. In real life it's deadly.

What if I think life isn't worth living?

How can you tell? Moods and feelings change. Every bad situation is temporary. End it all? Try life. You can always change your mind. But wait until you've lived at least half of it. At age forty, let's say, reexamine your life.

And then ask yourself the ultimate question.

Was it worth it after all?

Strange as it may seem to you now, in almost all cases the person says yes. You better believe it!

In the meantime?
TRY courage.

"Courage is an ability to dispose of self-pity and wallowing. You have to look beyond yourself. Courage is not, in any way, self-centered *except* it is self-confident. The courageous person says, 'It's o.k. I can beat this.' "

—Monica Dickens
(*The Boston Globe*, May 8, 1984.)

GO FOR IT.

2

What to do if you or a friend needs help

Do you have a right to feel bad?

In *The Right to Feel Bad—Coming to Terms with Normal Depression* (Dial Press, 1984), Lesley Hazleton writes:

> To be fully alive means to experience the full range of emotions, to struggle with the downs as well as to enjoy the ups. Life is certainly difficult and even unpredictable—full of meaning and purpose at one time and utterly meaningless and purposeless at another, sometimes so desirable that we wish to freeze it at a certain point and remain there forever, and at other times so undesirable that we may find ourselves wishing we had never been born. But it also has its own dynamics. There is no real happiness without the experience of depression to balance it. If we are not capable of depression, we are not capable of happiness either. In a very real sense, depression keeps us alive.

I bet you never thought of depression this way. I recommend Lesley Hazleton's book.

Are you feeling depressed?

Feeling bad, down, or miserable is one of humankind's most common ailments. We are not talking about people who are depressed for weeks—even months at a time. That could be a sign of a serious emotional disturbance.

This is about the ordinary depression that strikes everyone from time to time. But some of us suffer from it more often than do others. We won't dwell on temporary upsets such as grief upon the death of a loved one, or a bad mood. Those are reality situations that don't usually last long and don't cause symptoms like fears and physical problems.

The depressions we are concerned about here are the result of irrational ideas, such as blaming yourself for something you were not responsible for—all the "should ofs," "could ofs," "would ofs" in your life. Mainly, depressions occur because for one reason or another you feel inferior. You often or relentlessly compare yourself unfavorably with others.

Sure, there are always some people who are luckier, richer, more handsome, or smarter than you are.

Yet, did you ever think about this? Each person is unique. There is no one in the world who is exactly like you. Could it be that we are all on earth for a special mission or purpose? The great Eleanor Roosevelt once said, "No one can make you feel inferior without your consent." So, if you want to avoid depression, you must begin to feel better about yourself. Of course, this is easier said than done.

It's important to deal with depressions because they can lead to serious problems like headaches, backaches, fears, obsessions, nightmares, insomnia, or a chronic state of feeling inferior. There is hardly anything more exhausting than feeling inferior. (Some of you now know why you are tired most of the time.)

A lot of people try to solve feelings of depression in the wrong way.

They eat too much or too little.

They think alcohol or drugs can numb those feelings.

These may make you feel good for a little while, and then you feel worse than ever. You have a hangover, you feel bloated, terrible, alone, miserable, and broke!

What should you do if you're feeling depressed? Start by learning something new.

Need some examples?

Find in a dictionary three words of which you never knew the meaning. Read an article in a magazine you wouldn't ordinarily read. Get someone to teach you a new game, trick, or how to prepare a meal you haven't tried before. You might write down ten good things about yourself. And, if you can't think of anything else, call up a friend and ask what's new. (If the friend says nothing is new, hang up right away and call someone else.)

THERE IS HARDLY ANYTHING MORE ENERGIZING THAN LEARNING SOMETHING NEW. IT'S THE FIRST STEP IN GETTING OUT OF A DEPRESSION.

Here are some other suggestions to get you started.

1. Write a letter to someone who would be surprised to hear from you.

2. Go to a park, a museum, a play, or somewhere you rarely think of going.

3. Watch a program on TV that you wouldn't ordinarily watch—like a PBS documentary.

4. Go see a serious movie.

5. Don't watch TV for a whole day (better yet don't watch for a whole week). Find out what radio has to offer *aside from* your favorite music.

6. Bake bread or cookies from scratch.

7. Take a warm bath.

8. Or a cold shower.

9. Write down all the things you really like to do. Don't stop until you've written down at least a number equivalent to your age. If you are seventeen-years-old you should be able to write seventeen things you really enjoy—if you're eighteen, write down eighteen things, etc. Then, without giving it much thought, *do* one of the things on your list.

10. Daydream without feeling guilty.

11. Fix or build something.

12. Write a haiku (a 17-syllable poem arranged in three lines of 5, 7, and 5 syllables).

13. Purchase a magazine you haven't read before, like *Ms.*, *Rolling Stone*, *Psychology Today*, or *Seventeen* and read at least two articles in it.

14. Create your own psychodrama. Act out a *scene* for at least twenty minutes that you would like to play in real life. Be very animated and enthusiastic.

15. Get a pet.

16. Munch a carrot very slowly.

17. Make a decision to collect something (stamps, coins, cactus plants).

18. If nothing else works, try exercise.

It's a start. Of course we know that in the long run there is no substitute for feeling good about yourself through having a sense of purpose or mission in your life . . . a sense that life is worthwhile because your life is meaningful!

IF YOU HAVE AN INTEREST,
PEOPLE WILL BE INTERESTED IN YOU.
IF YOU ARE DEPRESSED,
YOU WILL BE DEPRESSING TO BE WITH.

You'll start feeling better when you put a little effort into learning something new; when it feels good to do something for someone else; when you begin to plan ahead instead of worrying ahead; and best of all when you don't have to compare yourself to anyone else.

How does feeling better feel? Energized and optimistic.

If you've been depressed for a long time

. . . especially if you are not sure why. . . .

Get yourself a complete medical examination; something may be physically wrong with you which affects your mental state. Then see a psychiatrist. Medication could help, but it's rarely the whole answer. Get into therapy (with a psychologist or a social worker). You may be able to confide in a professional even better than someone you know. They are trained to listen without taking revenge or getting hurt. We can't always say that of friends. A warning—don't stay with a therapist you don't like. Think twice about continuing to see someone if you haven't experienced a significant improvement after about ten sessions. I'm not saying quit therapy, but I'm saying that research in this field suggests that for most people some improvement is evident early in treatment. In addition, read carefully the sections of this book that are pertinent to you.

What to say when you are leaving
a depressed person

"You can count on me."
Shake hands or embrace and say with a smile . . .
"Hey, just because you are unhappy is no excuse to make
yourself unhappier."

Are you lonely?

The loneliness that is most painful is when you feel desperate—when it reflects a low self-esteem. The worst of it is when you begin feeling hopeless and alone.

Strangely enough, the loneliest people often feel the most desperate when they are in crowds. Some of the loneliest people I know are married and have families.

Loneliness is a state of mind. Well-adjusted people often enjoy being alone—even savor the precious moments when they are alone, to read, reflect, or just relax. It is their choice.

It's a different matter if you are alone without wanting to be.

Here too, it's a state of mind. Being alone, however, can always be put to good use. There are lots of things you could do when you are by yourself.

> Reading is the best. Also writing—keeping a diary.
> Being nice to your parents—or little kids. Offer to fix meals for the family.
> Be nice to yourself.
>> Eat well, dress well.
>> Treat yourself to leisurely baths.
> Clean your room.
> And you know what? It's o.k. to talk to yourself. (You can figure out a lot of things that way!)
> Call a cousin whose company you enjoy and suggest getting together.
> Plan a strategy for meeting people.
>> Volunteer work
>> A hobby
>> A club

IF YOU SHOW INTEREST IN OTHERS, OTHERS WILL BE INTERESTED IN YOU.

I know, I know—all this is easier said than done.

All the excuses
   No transportation
   No money
   I'm not attractive (There is someone for everyone.)

For some people loneliness will last a long time.
   (I was lonely most of my childhood. I wasn't good at athletics. Kids made fun of me because I was a redhead and I was clumsy with everything. I survived by daydreaming and reading books. And then as I got older, in the late teens, I went to libraries and museums where I talked to people and there met one of my best friends.)
   See next under "Things to do" a list of books to read and tapes to study while you are passing from this loneliness stage into a pleasurable aloneness.
   Sure, some of you are not into reading.
   That's o.k.
   You could move into fitness
      Exercise
      Build your body
   (You could still read a bit, instead of watching "all that" TV.) Learn a martial art such as aikido or Tai Chi. (If you stick with it, you'll feel better.)
   Experiment with meditation or yoga.
   You could even find out in depth what your religion is all about. But avoid cults. You can usually tell if it's a cult by the following characteristics (no matter how nice they are to you and how much they say they love and care about you):
   There is a leader who is supposedly always right. You give up your right to make up your own mind.

They have a philosophy that the end justifies the means.

You are expected to believe on faith and not think critically.

They encourage you to break relations with your parents.

A review! And three messages!

Loneliness is a temporary state.

Use the time to be nice to yourself.

Don't be mean to your parents.

It's nobody's fault that you are lonely.

Almost all parents mean well; those who don't are emotionally crippled.

Message one:

Take emotional and intellectual risks.

Unless you are willing to risk rejection, you won't have the chance for acceptance.

Message two:

Try to do the right thing for yourself.

You can't live according to other people's expectations.

Message three:

If you feel attractive, you'll attract people.

If you feel unattractive, you'll give off bad vibrations.

Things to do

You might start off by reading my *Teen Age Survival Book* (Times Books). It's for people who don't like to read much, but it could be a real turn on. For those who are into reading, try:

Whoever Said Life Was Fair, by Sara Kay Cohen.

The Aquarian Conspiracy, by Marilyn Ferguson.

When Bad Things Happen to Good People,
by Harold S. Kushner.

Feeling Good: The New Mood Therapy,
by David Burns.

Love Is Letting Go of Fear, by Gerald G. Jampolsky.

For novels that deal with the purpose of life, try:

Illusions, by Richard Bach.

The Color Purple, by Alice Walker.

The Snow Leopard, by Peter Matthiessen.

The Book of Laughter and Forgetting,
   by Milan Kundera.

Zen and the Art of Motorcycle Maintenance,
   by Robert Persig.

Siddhartha, by Herman Hesse.

Razor's Edge, by Somerset Maugham.

I would also recommend novels by Judy Blume, Kurt Vonnegut, Saul Bellow, Virginia Woolf, Amos Oz, I.B. Singer, Ernest Hemingway. (Ask your young adult librarian for suggestions.)

Russell Baker's autobiography, *Growing Up*, is inspirational. So is Eudora Welty's, *One Writer's Beginnings*. *An Orphan in History*, by Paul Cowan, could be important for anyone concerned about Jewish identity.

Don't feel like reading?

Get the magazine *Psychology Today*.

It always lists self-help tapes. Try ordering ones by Albert Ellis, David Burns, William Glasser, Rollo May, Jack Gibb, and Jean Houston. Look at the titles and decide which are most appropriate for your present situation.

Hooked on drugs or alcohol?

No matter what your problem is you can't solve it with alcohol, speed, coke, or grass. Even if you remain functional, you'll become less productive, as well as nasty to people who care about you. You'll spoil any chances of a good sex life—to say nothing of an intimate relationship. (Did you know that most males have their first experiences of being impotent after having drunk too much or taken drugs?)

People who are hooked characteristically
  —lie a lot
  —can't be trusted
  —are over-confident ("Don't worry, I can handle it.")
  —have poor judgment (That's why it's so dangerous for
     them to drive.)

If you can't stop on your own (or your friend can't), a Crisis Intervention Clinic will inform you where you can get help. Once you are addicted, or a chronic user of any drug, it is extremely difficult to stop without professional support. Getting help is an act of courage. Not getting it leads to despair and hurting the people you *should* care about the most.

Here is something else you must know. Just getting off the stuff will not automatically solve any of your problems. You'll still need the time, patience, energy, and motivation to make friends and develop interests. The most difficult period is the three or four weeks after stopping. This is a period of high anxiety and tension. This is the crucial time to learn something new, discover a hobby, try a new sport, exercise a lot, get involved in helping others who are worse off than you are. And, above all, don't expect to be perfect (you'll make mistakes), and, indeed, don't expect anyone to appreciate what you are trying to accomplish.

Learning to cope with this transitional period of anxiety is just as important as stopping substance abuse—otherwise you may start again.

If you don't like the way you look

Maybe you *are* too fat or too skinny or too tall or too short, or some part of you is not just "right," thighs, nose, breasts, penis. Maybe it's your imagination or lack of information. Perhaps you can't change anything about your appearance, but you can change your attitude about it.

This is the first thing you need to know. People who accept themselves are attractive to other people—period. It's not that short, fat, or "unattractive" people can't "find" a mate or a friend—it's that people who hate themselves and express it in being (not looking) unattractive, shortsighted, or fatuous tend to repel rather than attract others.

Look, if you are overweight, it's all right to diet. But it's not all right to literally starve yourself to death—a condition called anorexia. It's not all right to binge and then purge yourself (vomiting* or over-medicating with laxatives)—a condition called bulimia, or bulimarexia.

It's not an easy matter because most diets don't work for long. As M.B. and W.C. White have written in *Bulimarexia. The Binge/Purge Cycle:*

> Once dieting is initiated, the process and the end result become as important as the factors that led to the diet in the first place. Dieting provides a sense of meaning and purpose—a distraction from pain, loneliness, and insecurity. Many girls derive feelings of power from this form of self-denial. Others derive secondary gains for their vigilance. Friends are admiring and in awe of the self-denial required to lose weight. "Gee, you've lost a few pounds!" can create temporary feelings of self-esteem. There are often negative consequences as well. In their dieting efforts many young women begin to harbor obsessive, selfish, and competitive feelings toward other women,

---

*The use of the drug syrup of ipecac for this purpose is very dangerous to one's health.

gloating secretly when others are overweight. While they may want friendship, their preoccupation with body and their shyness keep them from gaining friends (or from being a good friend themselves).

The point is that even when you lose weight you still have to learn how to make friends.

Sometimes people worry about parts of their body for no rational reason at all. Males worry about penis size. Yet you can't tell the size of the penis by observing its non-erect state. Some penises that appear small erect to 5½ inches or more, while some that appear large erect to less. Besides, size of penis is totally unrelated to sexual gratification.

Vagina too small? No such thing. You could be psychologically tense or tight, but it can't be too small.

You can easily blame your appearance or some physical "defect" for any problem you have, but it's not fair to yourself. Haven't you noticed that *personality* is more important than looks?

THERE IS SOMEBODY FOR EVERYBODY!

Are you bored?

Everyone is bored now and then. That's of no particular significance. It's only when boredom becomes a style of life that you have to get off your dead end.

There is nothing more uninteresting than a bunch of people standing around talking about how bored they are.

Here is a list of the most boring things you can do:

1. Run yourself down. Tell yourself and others how worthless and rotten you are.

2. Tell friends, when they ask how you feel, all the details of your rottenness.

3. Tell people you're horny.

4. Boast about things that everybody knows you haven't done.

5. Watch more than an hour and a half of TV a day. Have you noticed—the more you watch, the more bored you get?

6. Talk about only one subject (sports, girls, boys). It's o.k. to have one main interest but, if that's all you talk about, people won't listen.

7. Always come across as pollyannaish (Oh, everything is wonderful!), or cynical and sarcastic.

8. Relentlessly tell people you're tired.

9. Talk too much. It's not as boring to talk too little—as long as you participate by listening.

10. Be sure of everything.

11. Complain a lot (ugh!)

12. Be paranoid and suspicious of everyone's motives, always thinking, "What do you want to know for, anyway?"

13. Relate to people without ever risking being intimate (which also means without risking rejection).

14. Be super-dependent on what other people think of you. They get the message that they can't talk frankly with you.

15. Begin your approach to people by saying, "I don't want to trouble you, bore you, take up too much of your time." It's fake humility.

16. Unwilling to try new experiences.

17. Be a super-miser. You don't want to do the most interesting things because you "can't afford it." It will be forever before you can afford it.

18. Persistently analyze the motives of everyone's behavior.

19. Be a gossip. (Super boring.)

20. Nearly always wait to be asked; hardly ever ask.

21. Almost always be serious and humorless; or almost never be serious and always kid around.

22. Relieve tension *mainly* with drugs or alcohol.

23. Almost never tolerate being alone.

24. Lead an unexamined life.

25. Spoil other people's stories (because you've said, thought, or heard them before).

26. Trust no one; or trust everybody.

27. Announce how self-sacrificing you are and what ungrateful slobs the rest are.

28. Complain that there's nothing to do; or talk endlessly of future plans that usually don't pan out. . . .

How to move out of boredom

The process of not doing anything is exhausting. A big disadvantage of being bored is that it's very tiring. It's no accident that when employers really want something done, they ask their busiest employee to do it. The more you are doing, the more alert you are, and the more time you have to do all the things you want to do.

By the way, when you are bored you need to be especially careful about taunting, tormenting, and hurting other people. Boredom is often one of the biggest factors in senseless delinquent acts and other evils.

The best medicine for *getting out* of boredom is to do or learn something new or different. This will give you a first-class rush, which you can then seize on to keep going.

You'll become alert, energized, stimulated, and more confident, too. Now is the time to do things: it doesn't matter whether it's to clean house, get a ball game started, finish a homework assignment, bake a cake, do all the odd jobs you've been putting off, or finally start the big project you've been dreaming about.

While it may seem difficult to get out of a bored state, if you are willing to take a chance and follow the suggestions below, it may not be as hard as you think.

—Go to the refrigerator or cupboard (many of you do this anyway when you are bored or upset) and eat or drink something with sugar in it. You'll feel better, but the physical effect will last only about two minutes. Ordinarily you might want to eat more and more, but then you might end up feeling worse than when you started. Here's the gimmick: Once you have taken something sweet you have two minutes to learn or do something new or different.

—Read an article that will give you some new information.

—Prepare a dish you haven't made before and try it out on somebody.

—Buy something you can't quite afford but that you've been wanting for a long time. I'm not talking about going on a buying spree, which is useless and usually results in guilt feelings, or about compulsive buying (which is a neurotic symptom, like compulsive overeating).

—Renew a friendship you've neglected for a long time. Risk its working or not working.

—Go out to an interesting place to eat.

—Let people know you are in a good mood.

Do you have a disability?

If you are not yourself disabled in some way, you very probably know someone, a relative or friend, who is. According to the American Coalition of Citizens with Disabilities, about 36 million Americans today—roughly one in six— suffer serious physical, mental, or emotional impairment.

Being disabled involves all kinds of difficulties—social, emotional, sexual, and, of course, economic. Part of the problem is that disabled people are often excluded from the mainstream of life by *the rest of us*.

As a psychologist who has worked with disabled people, I have some advice to people who are not disabled: Make an effort to befriend a disabled person. Do this not from pity, but with empathy and compassion, as an aspect of being a decent human being. Form your friendship on the basis of a common interest, or by helping the person to develop an interest in something you already enjoy. Once a real relationship has been established, don't treat the disabled person with exaggerated delicacy or sensitivity. This is likely to do more harm than good. In particular, don't hesitate to convey frankly what pleases and displeases you. For example, you may find that your new friend is "overdoing it," or misinterpreting your friendly interest for love. If this is so, the sooner and more decisively you straighten things out, the better.

Here is another important point: It's all right to start out feeling uncomfortable. Very few people can be fully comfortable at first in the company of someone who is blind, deaf, or cerebral-palsied. By acknowledging your discomfort, you can bypass pity, shame, guilt, rejection, or withdrawal. Talk about your discomfort, and then your friend may be able to explain, directly or indirectly, how to deal with it.

Now a few "messages" to a person who has a disability:

1. No one can make you feel inferior without your consent.

2. If you have interests, someone will be interested in you.

3. If you are chronically bored, you will be boring to be with.

4. If you have nothing to do, don't do it with anyone else around.

5. Most important: Our society does not give you "points" for being disabled. You need to work hard to make friends and to prove to everybody that you are a person first and that your disability is secondary to everything that is important to you.

You can't please everybody!

Are you the type who tries to please everybody?

Well, you can't. You can only *try* to keep your own life in order, not everybody else's.

What pleases one friend or parent or teacher may displease another. What you do isn't always understood or appreciated. You need to please mainly yourself—be your own person, and in that process you'll find that some people, not all (maybe not even many), will like you. People who try to please everybody end up pleasing nobody.

So, why not do the best you can, even if the best you can isn't good enough for some people.

What really counts in relationships is intelligence, imagination, character, luck, good will, and, sometimes, who you know.

So you might as well get to know people.

Are you very angry?

The legitimate purpose of anger is to make a grievance known. If that isn't done appropriately, anger can easily be turned into hostility, revenge, or even violent rage.

Just blowing off steam often doesn't result in relief because it doesn't take into account the person you are angry with.

It still is a good idea to count to ten before you express your anger, and sometimes it is a good idea to sit down and say— now whose problem is it?

I agree with Carol Travis, an expert in this area, who says that if the object of the grievance is not confronted it matters little whether the anger is kept in or let out. The recipients of rage also have hurt feelings. Silent sulking, however, is about the worst response. It's a passive way of expressing hostility which can hurt even more than coming out with what is bothering you.

Try to avoid turning anger into an attack.

Stick to the issue—don't wipe out the whole person.

Don't say, I hate you. Say, I am angry about what you said or what you did to me.

Anger is a legitimate emotion. Violence, as Carolyn Swift (another authority) suggests, is a response of weak, ineffective, inadequate people (villains) rather than of effective, strong, competent people (heroes, heroines).

A conference on anger, sponsored by the Institute for Mental Health Initiatives (Sept. 1984), concluded:

> Anger, appropriately used, can provide an opportunity to make grievances known, solve problems, correct an imbalance of power in a relationship, and restore hurt pride. Anger contains the potential energy for change. On the other hand, anger transformed into unresolved hostility can result in serious physical ailments, severe emotional conflicts, greatly diminished ability to function at school or work, as well as suicide.

Are you teased, or bullied, or excluded a lot?

If this has been lasting a long time, and especially if you don't have friends to help you out, you must do everything you can to put a stop to this intolerable situation.

Even if you have to be dramatic and say you won't go to school.

Tell your parents
    teacher
    principal
    counselor
    rabbi/minister

Say you are afraid of being hurt and it's up to them—teacher, principal, parents—to see to it that it doesn't happen.

Sometimes the worst of it occurs in a particular place like gym. Insist upon a change. Get a doctor's excuse, if necessary. Nobody should have to tolerate an unsafe situation in a school. It's supposed to be a safe place for everyone.

Sometimes a good technique is to approach the people who are teasing you (individually, if you can). "I would appreciate it if you would stop teasing and hurting me. I am weaker than you are and it's not fair that you take advantage of someone weaker. It feels really bad to be excluded." A direct approach, being polite and serious, often works. It's an act of courage, not weakness, to acknowledge that you can't deal with a situation alone.

These suggestions are worth trying, even if you think they won't work.

Do you feel empty inside?

. . . like there is nothing there?

It's a terrible feeling and it gets much worse if you do nothing, sleep a lot, or just mope about.

—Eating too much
—Drinking too much
—Pacing up and down
—Drugs
—Television
—Comparing yourself with others

These don't fill the void. The only thing that can is facing the reality. This will make you very anxious.

But take heart. The first sign of getting better is anxiety. It means that something *IS* there, that you are

EMPTY NO LONGER.

You need to take care of yourself. Go for
     a walk
     a swim
     an exercise

Call up a friend, someone you have neglected. Keep trying until you find someone who would be pleased to hear from you.

Talk about what's troubling you to a friend or some adult you think you can trust. Fill the void with ideas, alternatives, faith, in the possibility that life circumstances can change. Prayer, if you are up to it, can help.

You can feel much better even if nothing changes except that you have made an effort to fill in the empty spaces.

Do you feel overwhelmed by guilt?

Guilt is a good thing to feel if you've done something wrong. But there are two kinds.

Mature guilt helps you organize yourself and enables you to respond in a more rational manner to similar future situations or temptations. Mature guilt can enhance your self-image provided you don't overdo it and let it degenerate into

Immature guilt, which disorganizes and overwhelms a person. You can usually tell if your guilt is immature. It stems from an overreaction to something you did wrong, but more commonly from something you did not even do (perhaps it was something you thought about doing). More often than not, this kind of guilt is a way of expressing hostility against yourself, resulting in feelings of depression. At the same time the depression can be used as a weapon against the person about whom you feel guilty. Most everyone, at some time or other, suffers from immature guilt. The process of turning it into mature guilt can be a growth and a maturing experience.

**WHY TRAVEL HEAVY
IF YOU CAN TRAVEL LIGHT?**

Did some terrible thing happen to you when you were a child?

Tell someone you trust no matter what it was.

Let's say someone you cared about took advantage of you sexually. The first point you have to remember is that it wasn't your fault regardless of the circumstances—even if you agreed to it or liked it. All mental health specialists agree that it's never the child's responsibility or fault if an adult commits such an act.

Or maybe you did something wrong. Maybe you made a mistake. But now it's over. Why punish yourself more? The best way to recover is to admit your mistakes and talk it out with someone you trust. Forgive yourself!

If you had bad thoughts and something happened that upset you, remember your bad thoughts didn't cause anything to happen. You can not alter accidents, or natural events (like death), with your thoughts.

Forgive yourself and get on with your life. Your upset or depression is now harming a lot of other people (your friends? parents?). Not fair. What you do with your life influences a lot of other people whether you like it or not.

Life does not exist for anyone without disappointments, upsets, accidents, tragedies, and loss.

I like the way Earl A. Grollman expresses it in his book *Suicide:*

> In Hebrew there is a word *teshuvah.** It means "to return" and implies the opportunity of a renewal attempt, a fresh start, an ever-new beginning. Past failures need not doom a person forever. The willingness to build the temple of tomorrow's dreams on the grave of yesterday's bitterness is the greatest evidence of the unquenchable spirit that fires the soul of man.

*Literally, *teshuvah* means "return" and has come to mean repentance because one returns to God and to the right path.

What was the worst thing
that ever happened to you?

Now, answer this question:
Did, or
could,
anything good come out of it?
Did you learn anything from it that could help you now
or in the future?
Every mistake can become a lesson.
Even tragic events can become lessons.
Why allow the ghosts of the past determine what you can do
today?

<u>**Do most people fall short of your expectations?**</u>

Is it possible that your standards are too high?
- Unrealistic?
- Unrealizable?

Unreasonable expectations are the main reasons that
  —so many marriages end in divorce
  —so many parents are angry with their children
  —so many children are disappointed in their parents
  —so many love affairs break up

Think about it!

WE ALL HAVE OUR LIMITATIONS.

Do you have disturbing thoughts?

YOU ARE NOT YOUR THOUGHTS
YOU ARE WHAT YOU DO

You can at times get some insights about yourself from your thoughts and dreams and fantasies.

You can use your imagination to write poems and love letters.

BUT ONLY WHAT YOU DO WITH YOUR THOUGHTS
DETERMINES WHO YOU ARE

Remember, *all* thoughts, turn-ons, fantasies, dreams *are normal.* They could come to you voluntarily or involuntarily from your unconscious. Some are subject to your control—most are not.

Guilt is the energy for the involuntary repetition of unacceptable thoughts.

If you realize this, then it doesn't matter how weird or frightening your thoughts are. It is normal to have violent thoughts, imagining your friends dead. It is normal to imagine having sex with someone you're not supposed to have sex with. Your thoughts will pass and nothing will happen. Your thoughts will not control you.

But if you allow your thoughts to paralyze you, or if you permit them to explode into violence, then your thoughts are not responsible.

YOU ARE!

You say you can't help it. It may feel that way because you didn't realize that all thoughts are normal. They can become abnormal only when they influence

1. how much time you spend unproductively

2. how you respond to these thoughts by compulsive or impulsive behavior

3. when your thoughts are repressed and translated into symptoms such as fears and psychosomatic disorders.

(If you want to know more about rational thinking, read *A New Guide to Rational Living*, by Ellis and Harper.)

It's possible that just by reading this section, you'll feel greatly relieved. (Remember the Zen expression: "When the mind is ready, a teacher appears.") It is also possible for a bad situation that has lasted for years to change in minutes. Many people have experienced this. It usually evolves around

—an insight

—a love affair

—doing something useful

But this may not be happening to you right now.

If it's reached a point where your thoughts have become painfully unseparated from you, seek help.

THOUGHTS CAN CHANGE
AS YOU CAN

3

Sex and love worries and facts

Are you worried about sex?

For starters

I don't think teenagers* should have sexual intercourse. They are too young, too vulnerable, too readily available for exploitation. Ninety percent don't use contraceptives the first times they have sex. They don't realize that the first experience of sex is usually grim (almost no girl will have an orgasm—the boy gets his three days later when he tells the guys about it). But if you are not going to listen to me, use contraception. It's not romantic just to let it happen. It's stupid.

---

*A teenager is someone under eighteen. After that, make up your own mind about sexual intercourse.

Sex fantasies?

What about your fantasies?

All thoughts, all wishes, all dreams, all fantasies, all sexual turn-ons, no matter how weird, are normal. Often these feelings come from the primitive unconscious and we have no control over them. If you realize that, these thoughts will pass and nothing will happen. If you feel guilty about your fantasies they will recur. *Guilt is the energy for the repetition of unacceptable ideas.* They could be obsessive and explode into behavior. Remember, thoughts and turn-ons are o.k., but not exploitive behavior. It's o.k. to have thoughts of sexual seduction, but it's not o.k. to exploit someone.

Of course, the ultimate fantasy is falling in love with someone whose fantasy is falling in love with you. This sometimes happens in reality. The ultimate turn-on, however, is associated with intimacy—really getting to know and trust someone you are in love with.

(A complete list of books about sexuality is available upon request by writing to Ed-U Press, P.O. Box 583, Fayetteville, N.Y. 13066.)

Masturbation?

Masturbation is a healthy, normal expression of sexuality for both males and females. It is not physically harmful no matter how frequently you do it (males, by the way, do not use up their supply of sperm; it is replenished and available all their lives). You can, however, live a healthy, normal life never having masturbated. But it's difficult to be healthy if you feel guilty about masturbation. If you don't like it, don't do it. But it's normal—almost all males and most females masturbate.

It's always better if a behavior is voluntary. For example, eating is normal but, if people eat too much because of anxiety (not because they are hungry), eating becomes involuntary (compulsive). The same is true of drinking alcohol. But, if you must have a compulsion, please choose masturbation. Nobody has ever died of over-masturbating; however the leading cause of death in this country is related to compulsive eating and alcoholism (compulsive drinking).

Dying for a fake orgasm?

Some teenagers have been experimenting with putting a rope around their necks and masturbating—falsely believing you get great orgasms that way. Not true. You may get a pleasurable sensation for a second or two but most people don't realize how easy it is to lose consciousness when pressing on the neck. Sometimes just turning the wrong way will cause loss of consciousness.

But what is true is that every year more than 500 teenagers reportedly kill themselves without intending to do so in just that way.

Some teenagers have been experimenting with butyl nitrite (sold under such labels as "Rush," "Thrust," "Heart On," "Hardware"). You might get a thirty-second high—but may experience dizzy spells, blacking out, irregular heartbeats, and permanent damage to brain tissue. Butyl nitrite in combination with drugs like alcohol is even more deadly— last year several teenagers died as a result.

Really great orgasms can be achieved by masturbating (and fantasizing at the same time), but only if you do it without guilt. Masturbation can be relaxing and there are no harmful side effects, either for males or females. But, if you feel guilty about masturbating, you'll find that instead of reducing tension it will increase it. If you have an impulse to hurt or exploit someone or yourself in a sexual way, masturbate instead (privately, creatively, and with lubrication, if you feel like it), and you'll be surprised how your impulse will disappear. It may reappear, but now you know what to do. If the whole thing really bothers you, or you feel you are not in control, get counseling.

Homosexuality?

We don't know why people are homosexual, but about 10 percent of the population is homosexual. First thing to remember: A few homosexual experiences and having homosexual thoughts don't make a person homosexual. Being approached by a homosexual doesn't say anything about you. The only fair definition of homosexuals is: persons in their adult lives who are mainly attracted to, and/or have sexual relations with members of their own sex.

As far as we know, people don't choose to be homosexual—they just are. That's one of the reasons why it's not o.k. to be anti-gay.

There is nothing wrong with being a homosexual. It's just hard to be one in our society. If you feel yourself to be homosexual and you are comfortable about it, the only problem might be to "come out," or let people know—such as your parents. Some parents and friends understand and "coming out" strengthens the relationship. Some parents and peers don't understand and might flip. You may want to wait until you are past eighteen and in college. Even then it's not easy.

If you are unhappy about the possibility of being homosexual, I would recommend psychotherapy with a therapist who is accepting of homosexuals. Only with such a person could you get the understanding and help you need.

A book I recommend for anyone who feels homosexual but is concerned about it is *A Disturbed Peace,* by Brian McNaught. A recommended book for parents whose child is homosexual (or who are worried about the possibility) is *Now That You Know: What Every Parent Should Know about Homosexuality,* by B. Fairchild and N. Hayward (Harcourt Brace, 1979).

Pregnancy?

Pregnant? It's bad news, if you don't want to be, but not the worst thing in the world. Talk to your parents. Almost all will help. If you feel you absolutely can't confide in your parents, go to a Planned Parenthood Center or a Family Planning counselor. If you are clear about your opposition to abortion, go to a Birthright Clinic. It is your choice (according to the law) to make a decision whether to have an abortion or go through with the pregnancy. Counselors who believe in choice will not try to talk you into anything but will help you make your own decision.

More than a million women have abortions every year in the United States. But if you feel it's wrong—that's all right, too. You could also consider giving the child for adoption.

But here's the point: Don't do anything to hurt yourself because you made a mistake. Why punish yourself twice? If you've made a mistake, turn it into a lesson, not a tragedy.

Virgin rights?

Even though about forty percent of females and about sixty percent of males are likely to have sexual intercourse before finishing high school, virgins have rights, too (even if they have become a minority).

Despite massive societal support for virgins, this group is rapidly becoming more maligned and more vulnerable.

I believe that committed virgins should not be intimidated by peer pressure. Our society, for its very survival, depends upon people who have the courage of their convictions.

As a psychologist, I am frequently asked if it is normal to wait until marriage. I, of course, reply yes. I could be very sanctimonious and stop there, but I add: "If you are going to wait, I trust that you won't expect simultaneous orgasms on your wedding night. Otherwise you might ask yourself the question, 'For this I waited?' "

Sex is pleasurable
as an aspect of a caring intimate relationship. *But,* if I were to list the ten most important characteristics of a good marriage, I would say:

Number one is
love, sensitivity, caring, and respect for each other
Number two is
a sense of humor
Number nine is
sexual intercourse*
Number ten ** **is**
sharing household tasks together.

---

*Remember, too, people who boast the most about their sexual exploits are the biggest liars.
**Are you wondering what happened to 3, 4, 5, 6, 7, and 8? We need to leave room for your own ideas about what's important.

How can you tell if you are really in love?

Most people confuse sex with love. Yet there are people who have enjoyable sex and don't even like each other, and there are couples who love each other and their sex lives are far from adequate. About the dumbest thing anyone can do is to marry for sex—or "chemistry" as it is often called. Even well-intentioned people say things to young people like, "If you have sex before marriage you'll have nothing to look forward to in marriage—there'll be no surprises in marriage." I say, if that's the only surprise in marriage don't marry. It's not worth it.

Some say love is blind. I say it's blind for only twenty-four hours. Then you have to open up your eyes and see whom you are in love with. Love at first sight? Maybe—but better take another look. The plain fact is, if you feel yourself to be in love, you are. But there are two kinds, mature and immature. It's not difficult to tell the difference. Mature love is energizing. Immature love is exhausting. If you have an immature relationship—you have a tendency to be tired, you procrastinate a lot, you don't do your school work or your job well. You avoid your domestic responsibilities. (Me? Wash the dishes? I can't do that, I'm in love!) You have what is called a hostile dependent relationship. You can't stand to be without the person you're supposed to be in love with, "I miss him—I miss her (endlessly)," but when you are together you fight and argue most of the time. Mood swings and accusations of jealousy, even violence, characterize the relationship. (Some people even confuse love and hate: If someone beats you up or forces sex upon you, that has nothing to do with mature love; you may think it's "love" but it's really stupidity or neurosis or dependency or fear.) In an immature relationship, one person usually questions over and over again, "Do you love me? Do you really love me?" I advise the other partner to say no. You'll have your first real conversation that way.

Immature relationships are characterized by promises. "Don't worry honey, when we get married I'll stop fooling around with other women (men)." But, you might as well know now, a bad situation is *always* made worse by marriage. Immature relationships reveal insensitivity and selfishness by one or both mates; or one person is trying to meet the needs of the other and both are not satisfied. Love feels like a burden.

Sally says she has a headache, but Don is angry and replies: "You have a headache on my day off, you have a lot of nerve." In a mature relationship, Sally's headache is responded to... "I'm sorry you have a headache, honey. I'll get you an aspirin; there's always tomorrow."

Mature relationships are full of energy; you have time to do most everything you want to. You don't shirk responsibilities. When you are together you enjoy each other. You might argue sometimes but not that much. You want to please each other.

How can you tell if it's infatuation or mature love? The first month you can't (in the summer it takes two months). Infatuation and mature love appear and feel exactly the same. Then, when the relationship settles in, all or some of the above signs will appear and you will be able to tell if you are *really* in love.

Some good general rules: Sex is never a test or proof of love. You can't buy love with sex. So many females have sex because of the possibility of love, but many more males have sex because of the possibilities of sex. A large number of males find it easier to make out than to make conversation. I'm not anti-male, and I know that anything I've written about males is also true of some females. It's just that many males are programed by society (not born) to exploit females.

So until such time as men and women stop playing games with each other—women had better be "good" at those games!

Of course some relationships start out immature and with a lot of caring and effort they become mature (and some start out mature and drift into anger and hostility). The key here is that mature relationships are an evolving—not always easy or magical—process.

I like what James Nelson says about love:

> Love is "a many-splendored thing." It is the desire for intimacy and the willingness to be vulnerable. It is rejoicing in the presence of the other, a commitment to the other's uniqueness and growth, and an unwillingness to try to absorb or possess. Love is commitment to the wider causes of the other. It is friendship. And it rests upon a solid sense of the self's own worth and, ultimately, upon a deep sense of cosmic acceptance, of being at home in the universe.
>
> (From *Between Two Gardens*, by James B. Nelson.
> New York: Pilgrim Press, 1983.)

And consider:

> Two people love each other only when they are quite capable of living without each other but choose to live with each other. . . . True love is not a feeling by which we are overwhelmed. It is a committed, thoughtful decision.
>
> (From *The Road Less Traveled*, by M. Scott Peck.
> New York: Simon & Schuster, 1978.)

Dying for love?

Don't!

If you really love someone—your parents, your friends—don't kill yourself. No matter how they treated you—if your love at any time was real, I mean honest, good, why punish them so severely? It's not right. They don't deserve it. It's not fair. You don't deserve it.

When Scott Difiglia, a teenager from Plano, Texas, committed suicide because his girl friend rejected him, he wrote a letter explaining that he couldn't live with himself any longer. He concluded:

> I am really sorry for letting everybody down. Mom and Dad, I really love you a lot and I am really sorry. Thanks for putting up with all my shit for so long.
> All my love forever,
> Scott

Sorry, Scott, what you did had nothing to do with your love for Kathy or your parents, however sincere you felt about it. Real love *always, always* means you care more about the people you love and their needs than your own. Selfishness and self-hatred did you in.

Sure, we mourn for you, Scott,* but we mourn for your family and Kathy even more.

*See a powerful article about Scott in *Rolling Stone*, November 8, 1984.

Do I have to give up me to be loved by you?

This is a title of a perceptive book by Jordan Paul and Margaret Paul—a husband and wife team—both marriage and family counselors.

DO YOU HAVE TO GIVE UP BEING YOU
TO BE LOVED?
YOU BETTER NOT. IT DOESN'T WORK.

But it's not a simple matter.
Read what the Pauls have to say:

> Do you say "I love you" when you don't mean it? Make love when you don't feel turned on? Give presents grudgingly? Grin and bear the housework you hate? Come home early when you'd rather be somewhere else? Stay at home when you'd rather be out with friends?
>
> When you do what you do because you care—even when that means doing what the other wants you to do—you do not give yourself up. You give yourself up when whatever you do comes from fear, obligation, and guilt.

IT'S AN IMPORTANT MESSAGE.

·4

God concerns

Are you disappointed in God?

First you need to know that God can't do everything. We can't ask God to change the rules of nature for our benefit. God does help, however, those who stop hurting themselves.

Rabbi Harold S. Kushner expounded on these ideas after a personal tragedy in his wonderfully warm, deeply religious book entitled, *When Bad Things Happen to Good People* (Avon Books).

Rabbi Kushner says that God may not prevent calamity, but God gives us strengths and the perseverance to overcome it.

Meditation

Prayer invites God to let His presence suffuse our spirits, to let His will prevail in our lives. Prayer cannot bring water to parched fields, nor mend a broken bridge, nor rebuild a ruined city; but prayer can water an arid soul, mend a broken heart, and rebuild a weakened will.

(Gates of Prayer)

Yes, hope for a miracle
but as a Jewish sage suggested
don't depend on one.

Have you lost faith in your religion?

It's understandable if you think that faith can alter natural events and that belief in God means that God will arrange a good life for you. But God can't do that for you. Only you can try to do it for yourself.

It is, however, appropriate to agonize over this issue. Talk over with your rabbi, priest, or minister why it is that your religion hasn't helped you feel better about yourself. You might get some surprising answers.

A meaningful religious belief should have the role of helping you feel better about yourself and others.

This is what I think:

There is a way for everyone

People who want to
mock God
    say there is only
    one road to Him,
Lord knows, for Him
    a one way sign is a
    dead end
    leading to nowhere,
Lord knows,
    there are infinite ways to find
    your own way.

John Dunne, a Roman Catholic priest, theologian, and philosopher, suggests that we give up the search for certainty and go on a voyage of discovering and understanding. He feels the question is not, "Is there a God?" but rather "What is God?"

76 | *When Living Hurts*

If you feel yourself in need of prayer

When heavy burdens oppress us, and our spirits grow faint, and the gloom of failure settles upon us, help us to see through the darkness to the light beyond.

To You, O Lord, we turn for light; turn to us and help us.

When we come to doubt the value of life because suffering blinds us to life's goodness, give us the understanding to bear pain without despair.

To You, O God, we turn for understanding; turn to us and help us.

When we are tempted to suppress the voice of conscience, to call evil good and good evil, turn our hearts to the rights of others and make us more responsive to their needs.

To You, O Lord, we turn for guidance; turn to us and help us.

And when we become immersed in material cares and worldly pleasures, forgetting You, may we find that all things bear witness to You, O God, and let them lead us back into Your presence.

To You, O God, we turn for meaning; turn to us and help us.

(Gates of Prayer)

Meditation

Looking inward, I see that all too often I fail to use time and talent to improve myself and to serve others. And yet there is in me much goodness, and a yearning to use my gifts for the well-being of those around me. This Sabbath* calls me to renew my vision, to fulfill the best that is within me. For this I look to God for help.

Give meaning to my life and substance to my hopes; help me understand those about me and fill me with the desire to serve them. Let me not forget that I depend on others as they depend on me; quicken my heart and hand to lift them up; make fruitful my words of prayer, that they may fulfill themselves in deeds.

(Gates of Prayer)

*Or, day.

·5

If you are not getting along with your parents

If you don't get along with your parents

It is possible that your parents don't understand you.

It is possible that you are more adequate than they are.

It is possible that they don't care that much for you.

But in 90 percent of the cases parents do care—at least one parent does. They do love you. But sometimes they don't know what's right for you or how to express it. Sometimes they are so preoccupied with their own troubles that they lose sight of you. All parents have periods of time when they honestly don't understand their kids.

If the problem is not very serious ask them to read the section entitled, "A message to parents of teenagers—Don't turn off your kids." But, before that, you read, "A message to teenagers—Don't turn off your parents."

If you feel you can't talk with them or even if you think they just don't understand you, it's still important for them to at least listen to you. You may need to do something dramatic to get them (one or both) to pay attention to you. Cut out the following messages and leave them around where your parents can find them. Pick the time carefully. And then risk telling one or both of your parents how you feel. (Don't hold back anything.) It's possible that it won't work. At least you tried.

It's not that you'll give up. There may be other opportunities. But you may have to manage without parental support.

It's possible. Don't take revenge. They may need your forgiveness. Remember what we've said before. The best revenge is living well.

If you don't have the parents you want now, when you become a father or mother become the father or mother you would have liked to have had.

·1·

Dear Mom
I'm in deep trouble
I need to talk to you
I want you to listen to me
    without criticizing me
It's important

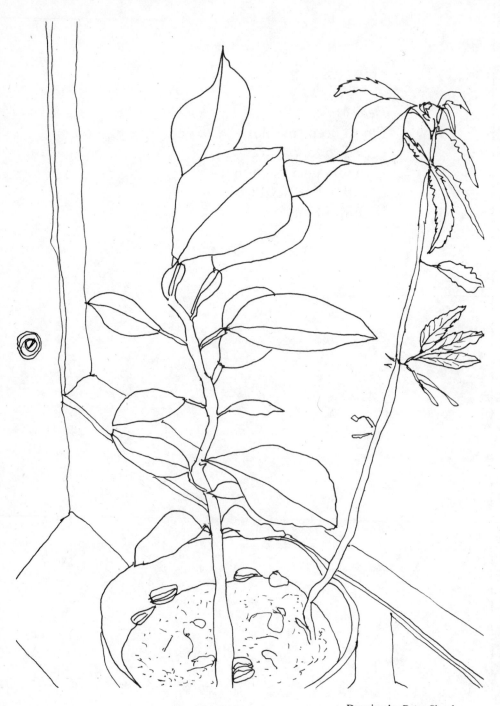

Drawing by Peter Siegel

·2·

Dear Dad
I'm in deep trouble
I need to talk to you
I want you to listen to me
   without criticizing me
It's important

A message to parents of teenagers—Don't turn off your kids

No, you don't have to compromise your values.

No, you don't have to shift from old-fashioned (which most parents are) to being what people call progressive, liberal, or with it.

Yes, you may have to improve your communication skills.

First there must be a recognition that adolescence is not a disease or a terrible stage that all young people go through. Many young people even enjoy their adolescence.

Teenagers need to be appreciated and accepted as part of family decision-making, including letting them in on problems—even serious ones like unemployment, fatal illnesses, and impending divorce. Teenagers feel rejected when excluded from family conferences. Parents need to be available for listening to the problems of their teenagers and for taking their problems seriously.

Advice

Never, never make fun or mock a teenager's love affair. Young people's feelings are as strong as mature adults' feelings, but generally of shorter duration. It doesn't matter one bit if you know for sure that it won't last.

Please don't say things like:

"You'll get over it."

"When you get older you'll laugh about it yourself."

"It's puppy love."

It's all right not to like your child's lover or disapprove of his or her friends. State your feelings, especially if the relationship seems to have a bad effect on the child's attitude or school work, e.g., if the child is using it as an excuse to get out of responsibilities.

You can simply state that in your opinion good relationships are "contagious." They make people feel good about themselves and are energizing. People in good relationships do well in school and can afford to be responsive to their parents.

Nevertheless, even if this is not happening and you are not pleased, you should be polite to your teenager's friends.

THE MOST IMPORTANT RULE IS NEVER, NEVER BREAK OFF COMMUNICATION WITH YOUR CHILDREN NO MATTER WHAT THEY DO.

This does not mean that you can't express how you feel about any situation. And try not to be known by your child as having a standard response to almost all crisis situations.

I asked my college students to recall a single sentence that most characterized what they considered as inappropriate parental responses to a serious problem that they had. A surprisingly large percentage of students, even those who claimed they got along reasonably well with their parents, recalled sentences like:

From mothers
- Life is tough all over.
- Count your blessings.
- Where did I go wrong?
- Go ask your father.
- Shut off the noise box.

From fathers
- Life isn't fair.
- Moderation, moderation
- For crying out loud.
- Go ask your mother.
- Life is too short to be miserable.

If you want to have a serious talk with your teenager, please don't start with the following expressions (which are guaranteed to turn off young people):

1. When I was your age. . . .
2. It's about time you (got good grades, straightened up your room).
3. That's not your idea, is it?
4. Wipe that smile off your face.

5. After all we've done for you.
6. What will the neighbors say?
7. Are you telling me the truth?
8. Act your age.
9. As long as I don't know about it.
10. Get off your high horse.

And please—in response to a teenager's concern—don't tell him or her not to worry. When's the last time someone said to you not to worry and you stopped?

You may have a teenager who does a lot of things wrong— they don't clean their rooms, they don't take their homework seriously, they watch too much television.

Try to make a point of dealing with one thing at a time. Concentrate on only one or two issues and, temporarily, let everything else go. This is usually successful if, at the same time, you try to improve the quality of the relationship by being involved in experiences together.

Telling teenagers all the not tos—
    don't
    smoke, drink, get high, have sex, stay out late—
doesn't help much
    unless we are able to help them discover just how to feel
    good about themselves.

Most children appreciate that their parents mean well and, in fact, getting along with parents is the best indication of good adjustment.

Not surprisingly, the area of teenager's disobedience is of perhaps greatest concern to parents, who often label it rebellious, spiteful, ungrateful, or spoiled. Concerns are magnified when the misbehavior occurs on a daily basis.

First of all, it's very rare for a youngster to be in trouble with his/her parents over just one issue: usually it's a combination of things. Many parents tend to talk too much and complain about the whole spectrum of problems instead of concentrating on just the one or two crucial ones.

Suppose that the main problem is a teenager who chronically stays out late and does not return at the prescribed time, e.g., midnight. After promising to be on time, the teen comes home an hour late without even having telephoned. The parent is waiting up, furious that promises have been broken, worried about the child's welfare. The child is approaching the front door, putting the finishing touches on the lie he/she has made up to explain the lateness (a broken down car and traffic jam are perennial favorites).

After having a good time with friends, the teenager's tension and anxiety have been building in anticipation of the prospective fight that awaits at home. The parents' own anxiety has built to the boiling point from hours of fretting, and from the memory that the child has been late practically every Saturday night for the last two months. In the fight that begins as soon as the door is opened, no constructive communication takes place. The parents' anger is interpreted by the teenager to be saying: "We don't trust you; you are a louse for making us so upset." Often the punishment which is administered is too severe for the offense. If grounding works, fine, but it usually creates even more dissension.

Next time, say just one line: "I'm very disappointed that you didn't keep your promise," and then leave the room. This is sure to generate guilt. (It should be noted that, if you had a prolonged shouting match with your teenager, any guilt he/she felt would be dissipated by the fight.)

There is nothing wrong with generating guilt in a teenager who has misbehaved—it's nonsensical to argue that all guilt is undesirable. Irrational guilt which overwhelms a person is not helpful, but rational guilt, which organizes a person and helps to avoid repetition of the behavior, can be a constructive force.

Let me state here my opposition to physical punishment under any circumstances. It tends to create even more anger and alienation and intensifies the conflict. Few things turn kids off more than a slap across the face.

Sometimes parents forget adolescents need models more
than critics and want their parents to respect their integrity,
privacy, and ability to be involved in family matters. Above
all, perhaps, they want love, so they can return it, and
information so that it can lead to self-acquired wisdom.

If your child shuts you out
anyway
   knock gently on his (her) door
and say softly
   "Honey, I love you. I want to talk!"
   or
   "Do you need a hug?"
   or
   "Can I give you a hug?"
   or
   "I need to give you a hug."
Persist even if the kid says, "Go away."

Don't wait for a crisis to tell your child you love him (her).
Kids, even teenagers, need occasional hugs and kisses without
any special reason (even if at first they seem not to like it).

Mention every once in a while, "Listen, if anything happens, you make a mistake—no matter how dreadful—I'd like
to know about it. If there is ever a crisis in your life, I'd like
you to test me. I'll never reject you. I'll help you, and if I
forget and don't respond appropriately you remind me."

If you tell kids they won't ever amount to anything, or they
are stupid, they might believe you.

Don't give your children the impression that they have
only one option:
   "If you don't go to college . . . if you don't
     pass math, you're doomed."
Better to say: "Here is what I'd like (or what I think would be
good for you). If it's not going to be, we'll help you find
something else."

Please don't make comparisons with your other children

and, above all, allow your children to express unhappiness, disappointments, and sadness without making them feel unworthy or guilty or that you lack empathy or understanding.

The main responsibilities of parents to their children are to
- love them
- nurture them
- promote their self-esteem
- help them turn their mistakes
  into lessons

so that they can become independent adults and still feel affection and love for you.

Please note: All parents who read this mean well, make mistakes, and love their children. Whatever happens, *blaming* yourself or your spouse is not helpful. Jerome Kagan, a noted psychologist, stresses in his book *The Nature of the Child* (Basic Books) that we have, in our society, greatly overemphasized the role of parents as *the* determining factor in influencing how children develop. Parents are important of course, but so is the fact that children are born differentially fearful, irritable, and alert. Peers and the media influence children.

Mothers seem to blame themselves for whatever happens. (They seem also to receive most of the praise if things work well.)

For mothers, especially: I rcommend they read Lynn Caine's book *What Did I Do Wrong? Mothers, Children, Guilt* (Arbor House).

A message to teenagers—Don't turn off your parents

One of the most difficult concepts for many young people to face is that their parents are really good people. It doesn't matter that parents tend to be old fashioned. They mean well even if they don't always make sense to you. Parental restrictions to you may seem like hostility—to them it represents their concern for you.

But, whether you like it or not, getting along with parents is more often than not an essential aspect of becoming a reasonably well-adjusted adult. (We do recognize that in some cases young people are better adjusted than their parents. For them it is still possible to manage in life, but it takes a lot of courage.)

Before we discuss improving communication with parents, consider the implications of the following idea:

Young people who don't get along with at least one parent are usually the ones who don't feel good about themselves.

So, if you've had some hard times with your folks lately, or especially if you feel they are not listening to you, here are a few surefire suggestions appreciated by almost all parents:

• Make it a point (or a sacrifice) to spend a couple of hours a week with your parents. Talk to them about anything, or just watch TV with them, but be sure to talk to them during the commercials.

• Every once in a while ask a parent who works outside the home: "How are things going?" (If he or she answers "Fine," say: "I mean, I'd like to hear about your job/business.")

• Ask one or both parents for their advice about something not too crucial so you can easily follow their suggestions.

• Experiment with telling the truth about aspects of your life that you have not been truthful about. If necessary, start by saying: "I worry that if I tell you the truth you'll be very upset" or "When I tell the truth, the whole thing gets blown up out of proportion."

- Clean up your room at unexpected times.
- Compliment them for things they do well.

Another way to conceive of improving relationships with parents is to embark on a one-month politeness campaign— which can be especially effective if you want something (a car, more money, more freedom for staying out late, almost anything except permission for sexual intercourse or a motorcycle).

Make it a point to be polite without sounding sarcastic. It may require some pretending. It helps if you can say at appropriate times:

"Good morning."

"Thank you."

"I'm sorry. I didn't mean to upset you."

If possible, at least once a week, without being asked, say:

"I'll be glad to take out the garbage."

"Can I do anything to help? I've got an hour to kill."

Chances are, your parents will flip. You might even overhear them ask each other if they should send you to a psychiatrist.

It's important not to fall into any of the traps they may set. For instance, their response might be:

1. "You want something from us." (Your polite response: "Of course. You always said I should work for something I wanted.")

2. "What's gotten into you?" or, "What took you so long to decide you're human?" (Your response: "I haven't been very considerate before. I'm trying to change to see if being considerate will get me anywhere.")

Let the experiment run for at least a month and then evaluate the results. If you have been working toward something you want, ask for it in this way: "I'd like to talk with you about something, but please at least hear me out before you say no." You may discover in the process that politeness makes life much easier for you, even if you don't get what you wanted. Politeness, however, is not a sure method of getting closer to parents—it can be a way of keeping your distance, which simultaneously allows you to discover your own way. You may decide to close the gap or keep up a polite relationship, but that's up to you.

Of course, it's like playing a game, and it sounds very contrived, but it's still a good way to break through a period of non-communication. It's a "pause that refreshes" and permits a more positive relationship to develop.

Did a divorce or separation—or living with a stepparent—mess you up?

Divorce or separation affects millions of children living at home or away at college. For a large number, their situation, as a consequence, was improved. Living with one loving parent was a relief after surviving years of two parents fighting, arguing, and even abusing each other and, sometimes, you. Unfortunately, many others from broken families have found themselves in really bad circumstances—and for a lot of reasons such as:

1. Feeling deprived.

2. Economic hardship.

3. A lot of added responsibilities that they are not too crazy about.

4. Missing the absent parent.

5. Being caught up in the middle—sometimes forced to take sides.

6. Having been their parent's best friend and confident, they resent another person coming into the picture. They feel angry and, in some ways, abandoned.

7. They were so worried about the divorce or separation that it affected their school work and friendships.

8. They feel guilty in a way which isn't constructive.

9. They are in a stepparenting bind that seems grim to them.

If any one or more of these or related issues has affected you, here are some things you can do and ideas to think about:

First and foremost, you must recognize that *it's not your fault*. If parents break up, for whatever reason, *it's not your fault*. You can't be responsible even if a parent in an angry, impulsive moment blames you.

Life may be tough right now. Life may seem unfair. You

may feel depressed, but that's not a reason to punish yourself twice. It's bad enough that you don't have the family life you want but that's surely not reason enough to do failing work at school, be rotten to the people you live with, or do stuff (like drugs) that is self-destructive. You need to resolve that you won't, of your own free will, allow a bad situation to get worse by hurting yourself. *Now* is particularly the time to protect yourself, be nice to yourself. Try at least to be polite to the parent or stepparent you don't like. Dislike could also change with more knowledge or even just forgiveness on your part.

In any case, however distant it seems, you will soon be working or in college. You'll soon be able to make your own decisions, live your own life, marry, have children of your own. The *only* way you can do all these well is to prepare yourself now. Get the grades you want, earn the money you need.

You may have to postpone some pleasures. You have to avoid inadequate "solutions," like alcohol. . . . Yes, you need to practice patience. You need to tolerate more frustration so that when you are old enough you can have the opportunity to do things better your time around. That's what life is about for a lot of people. That doesn't mean that in the meantime all aspects of your life will be grim. By no means. You can still make friends. Try to develop at least one intimate friend. You need someone you can confide in.

Develop an interest in at least one thing you can be passionate about. Be helpful to at least one person more vulnerable, more handicapped than you are. Make a commitment to at least one cause.

By reaching out beyond your own (perhaps even really bad) situation, you could be a source of comfort to others and, strangely enough, an inspiration to yourself.

You will feel energized!

6

What is the purpose of life?

Does life have a purpose?

Martin Buber, reflecting the philosophy of the Baal Shem Tov, the great chasidic master, suggested that every person born into this world represents something new, something that never existed before.

All of us have the task of actualizing our unprecedented and never-recurring potentiality and not the repetition of something that another has already achieved. Every one is unique for, if there had ever been anyone like you, there would be no need for you to be in the world.*

> Wow, I was so blown away when I read the Baal Shem Tov's powerful endorsement of *purpose* for each of us that it immediately reinforced my belief that I not only was unique and special but I also had a mission. And, while I would never be fully secure as to its exact nature, I *knew* that I was on the right track when these words came to me
>
> ### Created equal
>
> *everybody*
> *is*
> *unique.*

---

*See *The Way of Man According to the Teaching of Hasidism*, by Martin Buber (The Citadel Press).

Compare not
yourself
with anybody else

lest
you spoil
God's curriculum.

And what's more, my being a writer didn't depend on anyone else agreeing that I was one. If you are on the right path one person is a majority. (Marilyn Ferguson's *The Aquarian Conspiracy* set me thinking along these lines.)

Viktor E. Frankl has explored in depth the meaning of life in his remarkable book *Man's Search for Meaning* (Touchstone, revised 1984).

Frankl, a psychiatrist and Holocaust survivor, argues that the meaning of life is ever changing. One can discover these varying meanings in three different ways:

1. By creating a work or doing a deed—by some achievement or accomplishment.

2. By experiencing goodness, truth—nature, culture, and most likely by loving another human being.

3. By transforming a personal tragedy into a triumph—turning one's predicament into a human achievement.

Frankl concludes that, at its best, human potential will always allow for:

1. Turning suffering into an achievement.

2. Deriving from guilt the opportunity to change oneself for the better.

3. The transitory nature of life itself provides an incentive for action. There is never a good reason to be *stuck* in any suffering aspect of your life. The potential for change is always present.

Frankl's advice to all of us?

> Don't aim at success—the more you aim at it and make it
> a target, the more you are going to miss it. For success,
> like happiness, cannot be pursued; it must ensue, and it
> only does so as the unintended side-effect of one's per-
> sonal dedication to a cause greater than oneself or as the
> byproduct of one's surrender to a person other than
> oneself.

In this context Frankl is referring to "surrender" as giving of
ourselves to a loving relationship.

IT'S NOT GIVING UP, IT'S GIVING TO!

IN THE GIVING, YOU SHALL RECEIVE!

If someone asks you—what you are about these days
could you give a response
that approximates one of these
  • I'm in love
  • I'm an artist
  • I'm working for a nuclear freeze
  • I'm into my school work
  • I'm a big brother to a handicapped child
  • I've joined the Audubon Society
  • I work as a volunteer at the Children's Hospital
  • I'm excited about my home computer
or any combination of these which could change from time to
time.

Without a sense of purpose, life doesn't seem very exciting
or meaningful. That's why so many people end up filling the
emptiness of their lives with despair and addiction to TV, sex,
violence, drugs, alcohol, and passivity.

How does forgiveness work?

Let's take a cue from a Holocaust survivor, Rabbi Arthur Schneier:

> I can say that if anything, as a result of the Holocaust, I have been strengthened. Instead of just taking my energy and being bitter and resentful, I was able to harness this energy for positive bridge-building, with people of other faiths, with people of other ideological persuasions. That is the price I must pay for my survival.

Rage would be destructive and render survival meaningless. Forgiveness frees you to be your own person. It is energizing. It offers you another opportunity to be optimistic. You become the hero. Give it a try.

Start by forgiving your parents, or a friend, or a person you love a lot who has rejected or betrayed you. Often they mean well, even if they hurt you. Don't they say "I'm doing it for your own good"? Yea, sure! But sometimes they know not what they do.

Hate is exhausting.
    With
    forgiveness
    love is possible again.
And listen—

Just because you feel unloved now doesn't mean you are unlovable.

**If you can't forgive someone who did you in,
or if you don't like the idea of forgiveness**

·1·

First, pay attention to this statement by David Augsburger:

> Since nothing we intend is ever faultless, and nothing we attempt ever without error, and nothing we achieve without some measure of finitude and fallibility we call humanness, we are saved by forgiveness.
> (From *Loving Each Other*, by Leo Buscaglia.)

I'm not suggesting that everyone for every act must be forgiven. We may not want to forgive the rapist, the mugger, the people responsible for the Holocaust, but we should, for our own mental health if nothing else, forgive the people who hurt us without malicious or conscious intent. Or those who realize their mistakes and ask forgiveness. Who among us feels free to cast the first stone? How about those we feel we can't forgive? The rapist, the mugger, the murderer?

This is where our response or attitude counts. We may want to put some energy into punishment or rehabilitation for those who are enemies of society.

But why give the rapist the ultimate victory by punishing yourself for years? What for? Sure, you'll be hurt, upset, need support for recovery. But recover fully you must—you must shout out: "I'm alive! I'll protect myself. Enough of suffering. I'll help others. I'm determined that this terrible event will not destroy my life. I will live well!" (The ultimate revenge.)

·2·

A young friend of mine who made three suicide attempts before he was twenty-one, now at thirty-five very much alive, vibrant and creative, thrilled that he didn't kill himself, objected to my emphasis on forgiveness. He wrote:

> As I explored my spiritual being, I have succeeded in overcoming self-hatred by working with unconditional love, unconditional acceptance, and compassion. These concepts keep me spiritually equal to others and do not presume—which forgiveness does—that I'm better than anyone else.

His view was that compassion, not forgiveness, is the key. I'm not sure. Something to think about!

Is it ever too late?

It's never too late

    to try again
    to grow again
    to share again
    to risk again
    to feel again
    to change again
    to love again
    to be enthusiastic again
    to read Winnie the Pooh for the first time.

What does it mean when someone says to you "Have a good day"?

Nothing.

I like what one of my favorite people, Leo Buscaglia, says about it:

> I have always tried to define a good day not in terms of one in which all things were made right and comfortable for me but, rather, as a day in which I have been able, through some considerate and thoughtful word or act of mine, to make another's day more loving and special for them.

Leo Buscaglia has written several inspirational books. I recommend *Living, Loving and Learning* and *Loving Each Other.*

How is hope renewed?

When we talk about our feelings
When we confide in someone
When we realize that we can influence our lives
When we develop relationships
When we realize that all moods are temporary
When we do *mitzvahs** and practice forgiveness

How can you tell when hope is happening?
     You'll feel energized
        and
           optimistic.
When you realize we (the people who care about you) are not complete without you!

*Good deeds.

7

Fragments

More fragments of an autobiography

·1·

Sometimes it takes
    a death of someone close,
an awareness,
    "there go I
    by the grace of God"
(I could have been gassed in the Holocaust),
a recovery from a terrible illness or accident,
    surviving a catastrophe
or a "simple" mugging

to discover how marvelous it is
    just to be alive
    with all our imperfections

Some people are lucky
    They know this without
    being reminded by tragedies

·2·

My survival?
    a sense of humor
    a sense of purpose
    a sense of mission
    a sense of meaning
    a sense of beauty
    a sense of nonsense
    a common sense
        passion for *bittersweet*
            plays
            ballet
            movies
            music
            art
            novels
            chocolate and
            intimacy

June 12 is my birthday. Send bittersweet greetings.

What's a mensch?

First a mensch
Without aspiring to
be a
mensch
being alive is a
burden.

We all start out human
No way can we be more so
or less so.

We are at all times
struggling with the good and the bad
parts of ourselves.

Our free will represents the heart
of becoming a
mensch.

A mensch is someone who
aspires to be
a good person
and is
most of the time.

A good person is
someone who accepts the biblical injunction to
Love Thy Neighbor As Thyself.

This is not easy, especially for those
who don't love themselves
the best way to change
is by being nice to others
then you may at least
feel good about yourself.

If you bless others
you can then bless yourself
if you can afford to see good in others
you'll come to see good in yourself.
But there is still a catch

Not everyone is in harmony with your timing.
Not everyone is receptive to your kindness.

A really important obligation of a mensch is to do
mitzvahs.

A mitzvah is a good deed.

One does mitzvahs without intent
    upon receiving a return.
But mitzvahs *ALWAYS*
accumulate returns in your favor
eventually.

A mensch is a good person
who has faith in humanity
and expresses it with love and unselfish motives.

My mother (blessed be her memory)
used to say to us in Yiddish
Zug a Gut Vort—Est cost nit mare.
Say a Good Word—It doesn't cost more.
She was a mensch.
My life is a struggle to become one.
The hardest part of becoming a
    mensch is forgiveness.

18 slogans, poems, and things

"I have learned one important thing
in my life—how to begin again."
—Sam Keen

New journeys, experiences, and people call forth a *New You*. Why 18? In Hebrew, the word *"chai"* means life and its numerical value is 18. *Chai* is my favorite number.

1. The existential question is coming to terms with life—not death.

2. You cannot find yourself by:
- drugs
- dieting
- complaining
- getting laid
- jogging
- eating
- making a fast buck
- violence

not
- at discos
- bars
- cults
- movies
- races
- parties

nor
- in front of the TV

only by letting yourself
- be tried
  and tested
  in relationships with people.

3. An untested find (a sure cure, prejudice) soon becomes a farce or a weapon used against people who don't share your views.

4. People who feel good about themselves (most of the time) are not available for exploitation nor do they want to exploit others.

5. Not everything in life can be understood or resolved. All of us have some areas of vulnerability. Sometimes the best we can do isn't good enough. Some of us live in places where the winters are cold and long. That's why it's good to be optimistic.

6. Really marvelous experiences occur infrequently, are of brief duration, and are rarely on schedule.

7. "It is characteristic of wisdom not to do desperate things" (Henry David Thoreau).

8. You can get full with food but fulfillment comes only with love.

9. If you have a tendency to put yourself down, struggle against it. It's really boring to be with people who think they're boring.

10. Each individual is a unique being beyond the reach of diagnostic categories—an artist overflowing with the will and freedom to shape his or her own fate (fashioned after Otto Rank).

11. It's easy to be a hero in someone else's situation.

12. Intimacy
    is joyous
    and sad
    It is sharing,
    open-ended, and
    taking your mind off yourself
    momentarily.

13. In order to perfect oneself, one must renew oneself day by day (chasidic saying).

14. Love is where it's at
    and that's a fact.
       (A refrain from a not-yet-composed popular song)
15. All the way to Heaven is Heaven (St. Catherine).
16. Honesty is not necessarily self-disclosure. It is saying *only* what you mean (Sylvia Hacker).
17. Suffering may not enhance your life but recovery will.
18. Vibrations are real.

Thoughts and things to do for the next 18 days

Day one: Letting go of the ghosts of the past will permit you to have the life you're ready for today.

Day two: Let go of any thoughts that don't enhance you.

Day three: Give someone the benefit of the doubt.

Day four: You don't have to prove yourself to anyone today.

Day five: Say no when you mean no. This frees you to mean yes when you say yes.

Day six: Unselfishly offer a friend some of your energy.

Day seven: If you've wronged someone, ask that person to forgive you.

Day eight: Today say only what you mean.

Day nine: There is nothing you need to do first in order to be enlightened.

Day ten: Share a dream with someone.

Day eleven: Grow, by coming to the end of something and by beginning something else.

Day twelve: Set yourself a simple task and complete it today.

Day thirteen: Express your appreciation to someone.

Day fourteen: Realize that maturity is the capacity to endure uncertainty.

Day fifteen: Teach someone something new.

Day sixteen: Turn one of your mistakes into a lesson.

Day seventeen: Forgive someone today.

Day eighteen: Seek peace in your own place. You cannot find peace anywhere except in yourself.

"Be grateful for luck. Pay the thunder no mind—listen to the birds.
And don't hate nobody."   —*Eubie Blake*

"Life was meant to be lived."
                          —*Eleanor Roosevelt*

"When the mind is ready a teacher appears."
                          —*A Zen expression*

"Wisdom is learning what to overlook."
                          —*William James*

Repeat over and over again
  I shall either find a way or make one,
or, in Latin, if you prefer,
  Aut Inveniam
    viam
  Aut Faciam

•   •   •

And then say
  "I will be gentle with myself
  I will love myself
  I am part of the Universe."
                    —*Joseph and Nathan*

P.S.

Feel free to write to me. About anything—criticism, praise, yourself.

Perhaps you would like to contribute something of your own experience for the next edition of this book.

Include a self-addressed and stamped envelope for a reply.

DR. SOL GORDON
c/o Yad Tikvah Foundation
Union of American Hebrew Congregations
838 Fifth Ave.
New York, N.Y. 10021

Beyond Surviving:
Suggestions for Survivors

*Iris M. Bolton**

*Iris M. Bolton with Mitchell Curtis. *My Son. . .My Son: A Guide to Healing after Death, Loss, or Suicide*. Write to Bolton Press, 1325 Belmore Way N.E., Atlanta, Georgia 30338. $12.95 includes postage.

Hundreds of books have been written about loss and grief. Few have addressed the aftermath of suicide for survivors. Here again, there are no answers; only suggestions from those who have lived through and beyond the event. I've compiled their thoughts.

1. Know you can survive. You may not think so, but you can.

2. Struggle with "why" it happened until you no longer need to know "why" or until you are satisfied with partial answers.

3. Know you may feel overwhelmed by the intensity of your feelings but all your feelings are normal.

4. Anger, guilt, confusion, forgetfulness are common responses. You are not crazy; you are in mourning.

5. Be aware you may feel appropriate anger at the person, at the world, at God, at yourself. It's okay to express it.

6. You may feel guilty for what you think you did or did not do. Guilt can turn into regret, through forgiveness.

7. Having suicidal thoughts is common. It does not mean that you will act on those thoughts.

8. Remember to take one moment or one day at a time.

9. Find a good listener with whom to share. Call someone if you need to talk.

10. Don't be afraid to cry. Tears are healing.

11. Give yourself time to heal.

12. Remember, the choice was not yours. No one is the sole influence in another's life.

13. Expect setbacks. If emotions return like a tidal wave, you may only be experiencing a remnant of grief, an unfinished piece.

14. Try to put off major decisions.

15. Give yourself permission to get professional help.

16. Be aware of the pain of your family and friends.

17. Be patient with yourself and with others who may not understand.

18. Set your own limits and learn to say no.

19. Steer clear of people who want to tell you *what or how* to feel.

20. Know that there are support groups that can be helpful, such as Compassionate Friends or Survivors of Suicide groups. If not, ask a professional to help start one.

21. Call on your personal faith to help you through.

22. It is common to experience physical reactions to your grief, e.g., headaches, loss of appetite, inability to sleep.

23. The willingness to laugh with others and at yourself is healing.

24. Wear out your questions, anger, guilt, or other feelings until you can let them go. Letting go doesn't mean forgetting.

25. Know that you will never be the same again, but you can survive and even go beyond just surviving.